LEADING

WITH

EMPATHY

LEADING WITH

EMPATHY

Mastering Talent Retention and
Hybrid Work Dynamics

NOSIPHO SIWISA-DAMASANE

Contents

Dedication

I wrote this book to inspire young and emerging leaders to embrace empathy in their leadership approach. Employees and those who are led want to feel seen and heard. As a leader, you are responsible beyond the workplace, impacting their lives at home and in society. Lead them with care, recognizing that their contributions extend far beyond the bottom line.

Love

Nosipho Damasane

Award Winning CEO, Author, Speaker, Mentor and Coach

About the Author

Nosipho Siwisa-Damasane is an award-winning CEO and author with over 25 years of experience in executive roles across both the public and private sectors. Her distinguished career spans transport and mining coordination, specializing in ports and railway transport for both freight and passenger rail.

Born and raised in the rural town of Peddie in the Eastern Cape of South Africa, Nosipho's early life was marked by challenging work and a father who defied traditional gender roles. This upbringing instilled in her a resilient and courageous leadership style. As a child, she joined the boys from the village in taking cows to the dip, not due to her gender, but because of her readiness to tackle challenges.

Nosipho pursued accounting and worked for auditing firms where she completed her articles with Ernst & Young. In

1998, she made history as the first woman Port Manager in the world when she joined Transnet as the Port Manager in East London, Eastern Cape. She held a series of executive positions within Transnet before returning to the private sector.

As a turnaround specialist, change agent, and transformational leader, Nosipho is dedicated to people development through employee engagement and skills development. She is a trained mentor and coach through the John C. Maxwell program and has been personally trained by Les Brown in public speaking. Nosipho has authored two books on leadership:

- **FINDING THE WOMAN WITHIN:** HOW TO THRIVE IN A MALE-DOMINATED SOCIETY

About the Author

- THE INCLUSIVE LEADER: EMBRACING DIVERSITY AND EMPLOYEE ENGAGEMENT.

Nosipho exemplifies the principles of servant leadership, which are value-based and empathetic, and integrates futuristic thinking into her approach. She engages employees by validating their contributions to the organisations' vision through active listening and building strong teams based on honest communication. A gifted communicator, she excels in people development and career growth and leads in women's leadership development. She has worked and has been trained in South Africa and various other countries, including France, Belgium, Singapore, Rotterdam, Qatar, and the United Kingdom.

Introduction

Empathetic Leadership in the Modern Workplace

Empathetic leadership is the practice of understanding and valuing the emotions, perspectives, and experiences of others within a professional setting. It involves actively listening, showing genuine concern, and responding with compassion to the needs of team members. This leadership style fosters a supportive and inclusive work environment where employees feel valued and understood, which can lead to increased engagement, productivity, and overall job satisfaction.

In today's rapidly evolving workplace, the significance of empathetic leadership has never been greater. As organizations navigate complex global

Introduction

challenges and a more diverse workforce, leaders who prioritize empathy are better equipped to build trust, enhance collaboration, and drive innovation. Empathetic leadership helps bridge cultural and generational gaps, creating a more cohesive and resilient organization.

The post-pandemic work environment has presented both challenges and opportunities for empathetic leadership. The transition to remote and hybrid work models necessitates that leaders discover innovative ways to connect with their teams and foster a sense of community. This highlights the need for strong communication skills and the ability to create connections without physical presence.

Remote work can easily lead to feelings of isolation and increased mental health concerns. Leaders must, therefore, be proactive in checking in on their team members' well-being and providing necessary support. The blurring of boundaries between work and personal life has made it difficult for employees to maintain a healthy balance. Empathetic leaders need to set realistic expectations and encourage time off. Leaders must keep employees engaged and motivated without face-to-face interactions and this requires innovative approaches and consistent effort.

The post- pandemic era has shown that flexible work arrangements can be successful. Empathetic leaders can, therefore, leverage this by offering tailored solutions that meet the individual needs of their employees. This has resulted to the necessity for virtual communication tools to improve accessibility and inclusivity. Leaders who embrace these tools will facilitate better collaboration and idea sharing.

There is now a greater awareness of the importance of mental health and well-being. Empathetic leaders must champion wellness initiatives and create a supportive environment that prioritizes employees' holistic health. Empathetic leadership, therefore, not only addresses the immediate needs brought about by the post-pandemic landscape but also sets a foundation for a more compassionate and effective organizational culture moving forward.

The era of leaders who rely on bullying tactics has reached a critical juncture. Employees are increasingly demanding empathetic leadership styles, leaving no room for abuse and toxicity in the workplace. Today's workforce values respect, understanding, and support, recognizing that these qualities are essential for fostering a positive and

productive environment. As organizations adapt to these expectations, the shift towards empathetic leadership is not only necessary but inevitable. This transition marks a significant step towards healthier, more inclusive, and more effective workplaces.

Leading With Empathy

In conclusion, the rise of empathetic leadership marks a pivotal shift in the modern workplace. As organizations navigate the complexities of the post-pandemic world, the importance of understanding, compassion, and genuine connection cannot be overstated. The growing demand for empathetic leaders who prioritize the well-being and respect of their employees signifies the end of tolerance for toxic and abusive practices. Embracing empathetic leadership not only enhances employee satisfaction and productivity but also paves the way for a more inclusive, resilient, and successful organizational culture.

1

The Power of Empathy in Leadership

"Great leaders are not the best at every-
thing. They find people who are best at differ-
ent things and get them all on the same
team." - Eileen Bistrisky

This quote captures the essence of what it means to
be a leader in today's complex and ever-changing
business landscape. It is not about being the smart-
est person in the room or having all the answers. It

Leading With Empathy

is about recognizing the unique strengths of your team members and empowering them to work together towards a common goal. But there's another crucial ingredient that often gets overlooked in the pursuit of leadership excellence: empathy.

Empathy is the ability to understand and share the feelings of another, it is not just a "nice-to-have" quality for leaders. It is a fundamental skill that can make the difference between a thriving, innovative organization and one that's plagued by chaos, low morale, and high turnover.

Think about the most successful leaders you know. Chances are, they're not just brilliant strategists or charismatic speakers. They're also individuals who genuinely care about their employees, who listen to their concerns, and who strive to create a workplace where everyone feels valued and heard.

The Power of Empathy in Leadership

The COVID-19 pandemic has only amplified the importance of empathetic leadership. As employees grappled with unprecedented levels of stress, anxiety, and burnout, it is leaders who can demonstrate empathy and compassion that are more likely to retain their top talent and build a resilient workforce.

However, empathy isn't solely about being agreeable or avoiding conflict. It is about understanding the root causes of problems, building trust with your teams, and creating a culture of psychological safety where everyone feels empowered to speak up and share their ideas.

In this chapter, we'll delve deeper into the power of empathy in leadership. We'll explore the benefits it can bring to your organization, address common misconceptions about empathy in the work-place, and provide practical tips for cultivating empathy in your own leadership style. Whether you're a seasoned executive or a first-time manager, this chapter will equip you with the tools and insights you need to lead with empathy and drive your team towards success.

Why Empathy Matters

Truth be told, empathy is rarely considered as a key quality of successful leadership. However, cultivating empathy in how you lead those under your care can offer significant advantages. By being empathetic as a leader, you assist struggling employees to improve and excel in their jobs. You build strong relationships with them. Empathy allows us to feel safe with our failures because there is no culture of blame in the organization. Leaders get to the root cause of failures and poor performance by creating an enabling environment.

So, why aren't more leaders making empathy a business imperative?

I have personally encountered leaders who associate empathy with weakness, viewing it as a sign of vulnerability. In contrast, leadership by fear is often perceived as a demonstration of strength.

Empathy is frequently overlooked by leaders because it requires considerable effort and commitment. It is hard and it takes time and effort to demonstrate awareness and understanding. It is putting others ahead of yourself, something that is difficult given the competitive nature of the workplace today. It is not always easy to understand the other person's point of view and why they think in a particular way.

The pandemic has brought the need for empathetic leadership into sharp focus. The heightened levels of anxiety and burnout experienced by employees during this period cannot be ignored. Leaders cannot dismiss the fact that employees have had ample time to reflect on their primary needs by spending time alone especially during lockdown. Employees' expectations of their employers now demand empathy and the difficult conversations that are often avoided.

Employees can see through a leader who professes concern for employee wellness but fails to demonstrate it when it matters most. Understanding the issues that are close to your employees' hearts during times of distress is crucial. For example, how do you handle communication about mental health as a

The Power of Empathy in Leadership

leader? It is essential to destigmatize and normalize mental health discussions within your communication strategy. This also means that the implementation of the Employee Assistance Program

(EAP) should serve as a central resource for all matters related to behavioral health.

This period has also highlighted the importance of trust and psychological safety for employees. Only when individuals feel safe within a group, will they be open to discussing not just their strengths in terms of talent and skill, but also their shortcomings and what they perceive as each other's blind spots, including those of their leader. It requires a significant degree of emotional intelligence to receive honest feedback from your team about how they are led.

Leading With Empathy

The capacity for future growth hinges on your ability as a leader to stimulate an environment that encourages shared risk-taking. As Tom Peters aptly puts it, "A winning organization is one that rewards brave failures instead of celebrating mediocre successes." Only when individuals within a team feel appreciated, understood, and protected will they be courageous enough to try new things without fear of punishment for failure. Trust is the glue that holds such teams together.

A New Paradigm of Leadership

In the past, leaders were often expected to be stoic, decisive figures who ruled with an iron fist. But the world has changed, and the old leadership models are no longer effective. Today's workforce demands leaders who are not only competent but are also compassionate, who can inspire and

The Power of Empathy in Leadership

motivate them through understanding and connection.

This is where empathetic leadership plays a huge
role. It's a new paradigm of leadership that prioritizes relationships, collaboration, and the well-being of employees. It is about creating a workplace
where people feel the value of their contributions
and are empowered to do their best work.

But what does empathetic leadership look like in
practice? It is not about being a pushover or always
agreeing with everyone. It is about active listening,
and acknowledging your employees' feelings and
perspectives, and seeking to understand their concerns. This includes being transparent and being
vulnerable with them, sharing your own challenges
and setbacks, and admitting when you don't have all
the answers.

Leading With Empathy

Empathetic leadership is also about creating a culture and environment where employees feel comfortable taking risks, making mistakes, and develop their own decision making by learning from their experiences. It is about creating an environment where everyone feels a sense of belonging and feel the need to contribute their unique talents and perspectives for the success of the organization. The benefits of empathetic leadership are numerous. Research has shown that empathetic leaders are more likely to:

I.   **Retain top talent:** Employees are more likely to stay with a company where they feel valued and supported.

II. **Boost morale and engagement:** When employees feel heard and understood, they're more likely to be motivated and engaged.

The Power of Empathy in Leadership

III. **Increase productivity and innovation:** A culture of trust and psychological safety promotes creativity and innovation.

IV. **Improve decision-making:** Leaders who are empathetic are better able to understand the perspectives of others, leading to more informed and effective decisions.

V. **Enhance customer satisfaction:** Employees who feel cared for are more likely to provide excellent customer service.

Empathetic leadership is not a quick fix or a magic bullet. It requires a genuine commitment to understanding and connecting with your team. But the rewards are worth the effort. Leading with empathy results in a workplace where people thrive, where innovation flourishes, and your organization achieves its full potential.

Leading With Empathy

The Importance of Emotional Intelligence

Emotional intelligence (EQ) plays a crucial role in empathetic leadership. It is the ability to recognize, understand, and manage our own emotions, as well as the emotions of others. Leaders with high EQ are better equipped to build strong relationships, resolve conflicts, and create a positive work environment.

Empathy and emotional intelligence allow leaders to:

I. Accurately perceive and interpret the emotions of others: This involves paying attention to verbal and

II. Nonverbal cues, such as facial expressions, body language, and tone of voice.

III. Understand the underlying causes of emotions: This requires taking the time to listen to employees, ask questions, and seek to understand their perspectives.

IV. Respond to emotions in a constructive and supportive way: This involves validating employees' feelings, offering support and guidance, and avoiding judgment or criticism.

Leaders with strong emotional intelligence enhance the ability of to connect with their team members on a deeper level, creating trust, collaboration, and mutual respect.

Implementing a Turnaround Strategy

When faced with the challenge of turning around an organization, empathetic leadership can be a powerful tool. Focusing on the needs of your employees you create a more engaged and motivated work experience and employees that are better equipped to tackle the challenges ahead.

Leading With Empathy

Some critical steps to consider when implementing a turnaround strategy:

I.   **Show empathy:** Listen to your employees' concerns and fears and acknowledge the challenges they are facing.

II.   **Pull the teams together:** Break down silos and encourage collaboration across departments.

III.   **Create stability and give people hope:** Communicate a clear vision for the future and outline the steps you will collectively take to achieve it.

IV.   **Be vulnerable:** Share your own challenges and setbacks, and let your employees know that you need their help.

The Power of Empathy in Leadership

V. **Respect their experience:** Value the knowledge and expertise of your team members and seek their input on how to improve the organization.

VI. **Build trust:** Be transparent and honest in your communication and follow through on your commitments.

VII. **Walk the talk:** Lead by example and demonstrate the behaviors you expect from your employees.

VIII. **Create a shared vision:** Develop a vision for the future that everyone can rally behind.

IX. **Create clear accountabilities:** Define clear roles and responsibilities and hold everyone accountable for their performance.

X. **Engage and communicate rigorously:** Keep your employees informed about the progress of the turnaround and celebrate successes along the way.

Following these steps, you can create a more positive and productive work environment, even in the face of adversity. Your employees are your most valuable asset and empowering them to succeed and you can propel a turnaround of your organization achieving lasting success.

2

The Empathy Deficit in Leadership and the Rise of Quiet Quitting

Despite the clear benefits articulated in the first chapter, empathy remains an underutilized skill in many workplaces. A 2021 State of Workplace Empathy study by Businessolver found that while 91% of CEOs believe empathy is important, only 72% of employees believe their CEOs demonstrate it. This empathy deficit has significant consequences, contributing to issues like low morale, disengagement, and even the phenomenon of "quiet quitting" – where employees do the bare minimum to avoid being fired.

Quiet quitting is not just a trend; it's a symptom of a deeper malaise within the workplace. Employees who feel undervalued, unheard, and unsupported are less likely to exceed expectations for their organizations. They withdraw emotionally, become disengaged, and ultimately seek opportunities elsewhere.

The good news is that empathetic leadership can serve as an antidote to quiet quitting. Leaders who create a culture of care and support reignite employ-

The Empathy Deficit in Leadership and the Rise of Quiet Quitting

ees' passion, boost morale, and drive performance. When people feel genuinely appreciated, they are more likely to be invested in their work and committed to the success of the organization.

From Transactional to Transformational Leadership

The old, transactional model of leadership, which relied on rewards and punishments to motivate employees, is no longer sufficient. Today's workforce demands a more transformational approach, one that inspires and empowers them to reach their full potential.

Empathetic leadership is at the heart of this transformational approach. It is about seeing employees not just as resources, but as human beings with unique needs, aspirations, and challenges. It is about building a workplace culture where people feel safe to express themselves, take risks, and make mistakes.

Transformational leaders don't just manage their teams; they inspire them. They empower their employees to take ownership of their work and provide the support and guidance needed to achieve collective goals.

The impact of transformational leadership can be profound, and research has shown that it leads improved organizational performance and an inclusive work environment, where employees feel respected.

The Empathy Deficit in Leadership and the Rise of
Quiet Quitting

Embracing the Empathy Advantage

In the following chapters, we will delve deeper into the principles and practices of empathetic leadership. We will explore how to effectively lead effectively in a hybrid work environment, overcome challenges like bullying and toxicity, and develop the emotional intelligence needed to connect with your teams.

If you embrace empathy as a core leadership principle, you can unlock the full potential of your team and create a workplace where everyone thrives. The future of work is here, and it is being shaped by leaders who understand the power of human connection. Are you ready to join them?

Leading With Empathy

The Neuroscience of Empathy

Empathy isn't just a soft skill; it is rooted in our neurobiology. When we connect with others on an emotional level, our brains release oxytocin, often called the "love hormone" or "cuddle hormone." Oxytocin is associated with trust, bonding, and cooperation. In a workplace setting, it can foster a sense of camaraderie and shared purpose, leading to increased collaboration and productivity.

Moreover, research has shown that empathetic leaders activate the mirror neuron system in their team members. Mirror neurons are brain cells that fire both when we perform an action and when we observe someone else performing the same action. This mirroring effect allows us to understand and share the emotions of others, facilitating empathy and connection. Understanding the neuroscience behind empathy can help leaders appreciate its importance and develop strategies to cultivate it in themselves and their teams. Engaging with others on an emotional level creates a more positive and productive work environment, one that is fueled by collaboration, and a shared sense of purpose.

Being vulnerable as a leader

Brené Brown, a renowned researcher on vulnerability and shame, has highlighted the critical role that vulnerability plays in building trust and connection. When leaders are willing to be vulnerable, to share their own struggles and insecurities, they create a space for others to do the same. This vulnerability encourages a deeper sense of understanding and empathy within the team, leading to greater innovation.

It is important to note that vulnerability is not the same as weakness. In fact, it takes courage to be vulnerable, to admit our imperfections and ask for help when needed. When leaders model vulnerability, they give their employees permission to do the same, creating a more authentic and supportive workplace culture.

Embracing the Full Spectrum of Emotions

Empathy involves not just recognizing and understanding the emotions of others, but also allowing everyone to feel those emotions. This can be challenging, especially when dealing with difficult or negative emotions like sadness, anger, or frustration. However, embracing the full spectrum of human emotions creates a more authentic and compassionate workplace culture.

The Empathy Deficit in Leadership and the Rise of Quiet Quitting

When leaders acknowledge and validate the emotions of their employees, they create a space where people feel safe to express themselves and share their concerns. This can lead to improved communication, and more effective problem-solving.

The Importance of Self-Care

Empathetic leadership can be emotionally demanding. It requires leaders to be attuned to the needs of others, to listen deeply, and to offer support and guidance. To avoid burnout and maintain their own well-being, leaders must prioritize self-care. This might involve setting boundaries, practicing mindfulness, engaging in hobbies and activities outside of work, and seeking support from friends, family, or a therapist.

Leading With Empathy

The Importance of Self-Reflection and Continuous Learning

Empathetic leadership is not a destination; it is an ongoing journey of self-discovery and growth. Leaders who are committed to leading with empathy must be willing to engage in regular self-reflection, seeking feedback from their team members and constantly striving to improve their skills and knowledge.

This might involve attending workshops or training sessions on emotional intelligence, communication, and conflict resolution. It could also mean seeking out mentors or coaches who can provide guidance and support. Embracing a growth mindset and committing to continuous learning, deepens the leaders' understanding of empathy and its impact on the workplace. They can also develop the skills and

The Empathy Deficit in Leadership and the Rise of Quiet Quitting

strategies needed to create a more inclusive, supportive, and productive work environment.

Ask questions and listen with empathy.

The term "empathy" is increasingly used in the business world. Forbes has stated that "empathy is the most important leadership skill according to research."

Empathy is the ability to understand and share another person's feelings or experiences. The capacity for future growth hinges on your ability as a leader to foster an environment that encourages shared risk-taking. As Tom Peters aptly puts it, "A winning organization is one that rewards brave failures instead of celebrating mediocre successes." Only when individuals within a team feel appreciated, understood, and protected will they be courageous enough to try new things without fear of punishment for failure. Trust is the glue that holds such teams together.

3

Empathy: The Heart of Post-Pandemic Leadership

The trait of an empathetic leader is the ability to listen attentively to their teams. As a leader, you are tasked to define the long-term vision that you have for the organization you lead. While mapping the future, you also have to prioritize the short-term goals of the entity for your employees to transform your plans into reality. Excellent leaders understand that their aim is not just goal achievement, but rather creating something meaningful for all people while accomplishing the defined set of goals. This

Empathy: The Heart of Post-Pandemic Leadership

is often achieved through the alignment of the employees' inner purpose with the goals of the organization to achieve great results.

The pandemic period disrupted supply chains and halted many businesses, but proactive leaders prioritized the health and safety of their employees over financial risks and shareholder value preservation. This shift drastically altered the order of priorities in business. Organizations that placed their employees at the center of their decision-making found that their employees responded positively. As a result, these organizations experienced a faster recovery in financial performance as the economy began to reopen.

Leading With Empathy

The biggest challenge for many leaders is their inability to understand employees' needs. Consequently, employee turnover has become a major issue for organizations during this period. Organizations that take the time to understand why turnover occurs respond thoughtfully to the needs of both current and prospective employees and they attract and retain talent.

According to the McKinsey & Company latest report, a record number of employees are quitting or thinking about doing so. More than 15 million US workers are quitting their jobs, which is a huge disruption to business. Companies are struggling to address the problem, and they do not really understand why their employees are leaving in the first place. Instead of taking time to investigate the true causes for the attrition, they are jumping to well-intentioned quick fixes that fall flat. They are bumping

Empathy: The Heart of Post-Pandemic Leadership

up things like pay and financial perks and bonuses without making any effort to strengthen the relations and ties between the employer and the employee. While employees will accept the financial perks, deep down they view these gestures as being indicative of a transactional relationship that reminds them that their real needs are not met. Michael Tatelbam, Vice-President of Human Capital for Villa Healthcare in Skokie, Illinois, reports:

"As part of my servant leadership work, I've been very focused on Stephen Covey's speed of trust concept: connect-trust-act. Dr Covey talks about the importance of taking time to connect with others, to build trust, and then move to action. Leaders (and others) tend to move right to action. At Villa, I've implemented Coffee Talks, a chance for me to explain the concept and live by it meaning more connection with our corporate staff.? These Coffee

Talks are limited to six corporate staff at a time. Offered monthly, staff voluntarily sign up, but there's a buzz in the office and staff wait and watch for the sign-up sheet each month. We all take time to share at the level each person is comfortable with. I talk about the power of vulnerability, that everyone has a story. As a result, the group realizes how we are more similar than different. Right now, only I am doing these, but soon we will expect our facility leaders to do Coffee Talks with their staff. It's extremely powerful in so many ways."

Employers who fail to invest in creating a more fulfilling employee experience will struggle to meet the new demands of workers for autonomy and flexibility. To succeed, employers must strive to understand their employees, who are seeking connectiv-

Empathy: The Heart of Post-Pandemic Leadership

ity, unity, and a sense of purpose. Achieving this requires empathy, compassion, and a commitment to effecting change in partnership with employees.

To gain an edge in the race to retain talent and build a thriving post-pandemic organization, companies must seize this unique moment to engage their employees in a more meaningful way. The major challenge for leaders will be to reimagine their approach to leadership. While effective leadership skills such as coaching and mentoring, which were relevant before the pandemic, remain important, they are no longer sufficient for the post-pandemic era. Employee retention drivers have become more complex, with new factors including the flexibility to work remotely, the option of a hybrid working model, or the possibility of working entirely from home. Organizations that fail to recognize this need may miss the boat. The problem is compounded by organizational cultures that remain hierarchical and maintain a "I am the boss" mentality, which are likely to fail.

Studies conducted by the Harvard Business Review, indicate that organizations that succeed in remaining profitable in a sustainable manner are those that take engagement seriously. The top three factors cited by employees in the McKinsey report were that employees did not feel valued did not feel a sense of belonging at work. Employees value relational factors, whilst employers are focusing on transactional factors. *"You'll never get the best from employees by trying to build a fire under them. You've got to build a fire with them,"* *Bob Nelson*

4

Building a Culture of Empathy

Organizational culture represents the organization's personality and character. It encompasses the way things are done, the unwritten rules that influence individual and group attitudes, and dictates the core values, underlying beliefs, and standards that thrive within the organization. It is the glue that binds everyone together and forms the foundation of all organizational activities. Mike Teke was my Chairman at Richards Bay Coal Terminal. Early days in my transition as Chief Executive Officer, posed a challenging.

question to our executive team: "If someone asked who you are and what you stand for, would we be able to answer that simply?" This question was tough at the time. It led us to unpack and understand our organizational culture deeply. Through this process, we realized that organizational culture should define how we do things, even those that are not explicitly written down.

Reputation is closely tied to culture. Some organizations establish a compact with their employees based on a set of agreed-upon values that govern how things are done, which constitutes their organizational culture. The organizations that successfully attract and retain great talent are those that "walk the talk" regarding their culture. Employees in these organizations feel positive about their work and are often fully aligned with the values espoused.

Leading With Empathy

The beliefs and values that guide behavior in an organization might seem intangible, but culture is inextricably linked to the organization's bottom line. At the heart of a high-performance culture is a communication strategy that centers on the workplace. Great leaders view

culture as a strategic priority rather than allowing it to evolve passively. They understand that culture is a defining element of the workplace experience. The key is to ensure that every employee feels important and included.

In response to the proliferation of digital technology, some organizations have established communication apps as tools to maintain their strategic focus and enhance workplace cohesion. This reality will extend into the post-pandemic era, where remote working has scattered employees across various locations. Executives need to rethink and leverage cultures that will maximize business returns by strengthening their workforce and enhancing the bottom line.

A results-driven culture prioritizes an internal communications strategy and tools that drive engagement and increase retention. Companies with a participative culture see a return on investment that averages twice as high as those with a less participative approach.

It is critical to measure organizational culture through a branch of human capital known as people analytics, with surveys serving as the starting point. At a more sophisticated level, people analytics encompasses HR data literacy, data analysis, HR reporting and dashboarding, data visualization, as well as research and statistics.

Leading With Empathy

In organizations where there is a culture of mistrust and fear due to a hierarchical leadership structure, conducting independent surveys is advisable. This approach allows employees to freely express their true feelings about the organization. Even when these surveys are managed independently, it is crucial that the results are handled transparently.

However, some organizations may tamper with the results to alter their meaning and present a more favorable view to their leaders. Such practices typically indicate a reluctance to change and often reflect an unhealthy organizational culture and poor financial performance.

A troubling global culture has emerged, where leaders sometimes assume absolute power and forget that they are entrusted with people's lives by creating unbearable.

toxicity. Consequently, their actions in the workplace inevitably impact the employees' lives outside of work. Some corporate environments are becoming increasingly oppressive, where employees feel silenced and fear repercussions for speaking out. This culture instils fear, causing employees to go to work every day like zombies, paralyzed by the fear of losing their jobs. With concerns about their livelihood, and family responsibilities such as school fees and mortgages, employees feel entrapped.

In organizations where this culture prevails, it has a paralyzing effect on many professionals. It erodes morale and has been known to destroy careers, severely affecting individuals' well-being and professional growth. Culture defines the character or personality of an organization. A negative culture is inherently unsustainable. In the absolute power scenario, great talent moves first. This group of people has options, they can find new jobs, work remotely, start their own businesses, or simply leave.

In such a culture, there is also the problem of individuals being divided into factions, each led by certain "chiefs." Being labelled as part of a particular faction can mean that, during leadership changes, you might find yourself without a place in the organization. This form of leadership is detrimental; it deprives organizations of valuable talent and skills, and ultimately undermines the bottom line. How can you dedicate yourself to education and hard work, only to become a 'henchman? Remarkably, those in such dictatorial leadership positions often believe they are acting in the organization's best interests. They tend to focus on recounting past victories, believing this will somehow ensure the future sustainability of the business they currently lead.

Building a Culture of Empathy

At its core, the absolute power paradigm is rooted in the belief that "I know what's best," and that those I lead would be "lost without my guidance." This mindset fosters the notion of being irreplaceable. The irony, however, is that graveyards are full of people who were once considered "irreplaceable."

I. Traits of a bad organizational culture include:
II. Absence of core shared values
III. Lots of gossip in the office
IV. Unhealthy employee competition
V. Absenteeism and tardiness
VI. No time for lunch for the employees and going home late daily.

A strong organizational culture is vital for your company's longevity and success. To build a vibrant culture that attracts job seekers and retains employees, you must be deliberate about the type of organizational culture you want to create. As job seekers gain more leverage in the future, a solid organizational culture will be essential for attracting top talent. To retain these candidates, the key will be employee engagement, which consistently leads to higher productivity.

Organizational culture in the digital age will differ significantly from what it is today, particularly with the post-pandemic shift toward remote and rotational work. In such environments, where employees do not consistently interact with the same people, maintaining a cohesive and engaging culture will be even more challenging.

To maintain a coherent organizational culture, leadership must commit to ongoing discussions about the organization's purpose, the pivotal role of em-

Building a Culture of Empathy

ployees, and the future direction of the company. Leaders need to understand the value of agility and invest in it. Organizational culture can either be your greatest strength or your most detrimental weakness. The key is to remain vigilant against harmful company culture and work proactively to address and change it. If the organizational culture is unacceptable, employee turnover will likely be high. Employees are often willing to accept a lower salary in a healthier, less toxic environment rather than stay for higher pay in a toxic culture.

The questions to ask yourself are:

I.   How culturally prepared was your organization to deal with the crisis?

II. Will the ongoing situation bring your employees together or drive them apart?

III. Will they see the organization differently when this is over?

Your answers will inform what you can achieve in the post-pandemic reality.

A toxic culture can be the downfall of any organization is like a disease that slowly erodes trust, morale, and productivity, ultimately leading to the departure of valuable talent and the decline of the bottom line.

5

The Essence of a People-centred Culture

In this chapter, I recount my transformative journey as the CEO of Richards Bay Coal Terminal, where we prioritized the well-being of our employees and created a people-centred culture that became the cornerstone of our success. Through initiatives like retreats, IMBIZO gatherings, and undercover work, we built trust, care, and transparency, leading to

The Essence of a People-centred Culture

zero staff turnover and strong alignment even during the pandemic. This approach not only shaped the organization's culture but also demonstrated the lasting impact of empathetic leadership.

When I was the CEO of the Richards Bay Coal Terminal, I initiated a transformative practice with my executive team: we would retreat for two days to focus solely on the well-being of our employees. This involved talent management and required significant time and effort to truly understand our people. Reflecting on it, this approach proved to be one of the most important tools for helping us, as a leadership team, to grasp our employees' concerns and worries. We agreed that we needed to be prepared to hear employee feedback and complaints, no matter how challenging. We recognized that we could not change the environment on our own as leaders, so it was crucial to create platforms for engagement with employees.

This was followed by IMBIZO, a regular gathering we held with all employees. We created so much energy and excitement around these engagements. Employees were allowed to voice their issues, and in this way, they felt heard and seen. This was done once a quarter and there were clear follow-ups on the views expressed and issues raised. This was also used as an opportunity to allow the sharing of ideas. Leadership utilized this platform to also communicate organizational performance, any new projects that were underway, growth opportunities and customer experience.

This was used as a "checking the pulse" exercise whilst strengthening the partnership. After these sessions, the management team had the opportunity

The Essence of a People-centred Culture

to check and discuss what could be done better or differently to improve the rhythm.

Another key factor in employee engagement is conducting organizational health surveys in the form of workshops at least once a year. This provides a collective view of the organization's current state and assesses whether employees remain aligned with the vision and mission. This approach helped us align the shared vision with our value system and organizational culture.

Transactional discussions, such as those about incentives and financial issues, were part of our approach but were never the key priority. We believed that money was not the only motivator. To understand the real issues behind the high staff turnover and low morale when I arrived at RBCT, I went undercover as a student from South32, one of our shareholders. I wanted to experience first-hand the underlying problems so I could integrate them into the turnaround strategy. I gained valuable insights by spending time with employees without them knowing I was the incoming CEO. They shared openly about the real issues, which helped me understand their working conditions and identify areas for improvement. By addressing these issues and making impactful changes to their daily lives, we were able to resolve over 90% of the challenges I discovered. This approach quickly fostered a strong sense of trust and became a key pillar in implementing our strategy.

When employees are the center of the strategy

Our focus was on the sustainability of the organization through its people. For us, people were at the core of everything we did. We understood that to achieve the turnaround of the business, our employees had to have faith in the leadership team. We demonstrated care for individuals and established clear outputs and accountability measures. There was no ambiguity regarding key performance indicators (KPIs) or what was expected from teams and individuals, including their Key Performance

Areas (KPAs) and career development with a clear succession planning process. This approach allowed us to shape the landscape and culture we aimed to build—a people-centred culture. While some might have initially thought this approach was a waste of time due to its tedious nature, it proved to be fundamental to our success.

As a result, when we were asked how we achieved our success, we consistently told the industry that it was due to our emphasis on trust and care for our people. We were transparent about the expected outputs and used incentives rather than punitive measures. This approach led to zero staff turnover and the creation of clear career advancement paths. The culture we developed not only endured beyond my tenure but has also become embedded in the organization's delivery model to this day. Employees embraced the changes because they were involved in the process, leading to a heightened sense of ownership and buy-in from everyone. During the pandemic, the employees

at RBCT remained aligned with the organization's trial-and-error adjustments to fit COVID regulations, thanks to the foundation of trust and respect between employees and the employer. Where there is trust, implementing change becomes easier. Employee attraction and retention are built on this

The Essence of a People-centred Culture

premise and reputation. Organizations with passive-aggressive leadership styles struggle to survive.

Glen Leibowitz has produced twelve traits of exceptional leaders that are critical in the pandemic phase and will be more relevant in post-pandemic organizations. It is getting tougher because of the demand or preference for hybrid type of work, and the remote working practices that will be ruling the corporate world in the post-pandemic economy. These leaders have the following traits:

I.   They trust you to do the job you've been hired to do.
II. They seek your advice and input.
III. They find opportunity to let you shine.
IV. They recognize your contributions.
V.   They have your back during tough times.

VI.   They challenge you to do bigger and better things.

VII. They express appreciation.

VIII. They are responsive.

IX.   They know when to apologize.

X.   They give credit where it is due.

XI.   They treat others with dignity and respect.

XII. Most importantly, they CARE.

The employees feel the Obvious Greater Value (OGV) when they know that they are heard, and how they are valued by their employers.

I attended a two-day strategy review session conducted by The Performance Agency, in October 2021, where I am a Non-Executive Chairman. The CEO inspired me when she stopped the review process and said, "People have been expressing a feeling of burnout" and "I would rather spend the time listening to them discuss how we can work smarter."

Where she really got it right is that she did not want to push strategy to people who are in pain. She chose to deal with the issues at hand, for them to absorb the strategic direction, they need to feel heard. This kind of flexibility comes with maturity and excellent leadership.

6

The Power and Perils of Organizational Culture

Here, we explore the profound impact of organizational culture on a company's success and longevity. We delve into how culture shapes behavior, aligns values, and influences both employee satisfaction and the bottom line. The chapter also highlights the importance of deliberate cultural strategies, the dangers of toxic environments, and the critical role of leaders in fostering a positive, inclusive, and resili-

The Power and Perils of Organizational Culture

ent workplace. As we transition into the post-pandemic era, the challenges, and opportunities of maintaining a cohesive culture in a remote and digital landscape are examined, emphasizing the need for continuous engagement and adaptability.

Organizational culture represents the organization's personality and character. It encompasses the way things are done, the unwritten rules that influence individual and group attitudes, and dictates the core values, underlying beliefs, and standards that thrive within the organization. It is the glue that binds everyone together and forms the foundation of all organizational activities.

Reputation is closely tied to culture. Some organizations establish a compact with their employees based on a set of agreed-upon values that govern how things are done, which constitutes their organizational culture. The organizations that successfully attract and retain great talent are those that "walk the talk" regarding their culture. Employees in these organizations feel positive about their work and are often fully aligned with the values espoused.

The beliefs and values that guide behavior in an organization might seem intangible, but culture is inextricably linked to the organization's bottom line. At the heart of a high-performance culture is a communication strategy that centres on the workplace. Great leaders view culture as a strategic priority rather than allowing it to evolve passively. They understand that culture is a defining element of the workplace experience. The key is to ensure that every employee feels important and included.

The Power and Perils of Organizational Culture

In response to the proliferation of digital technology, some organizations have established communication apps as tools to maintain their strategic focus and enhance workplace cohesion.

Customers are not only using multiple channels and devices—but often using them simultaneously!
How can a disconnected, proliferated business possibly hope to engage the digital consumer while attaining the revenue and operating margins that digitally born businesses take for granted? There is an answer! Orchestrating customer engagement centrally and holistically is the answer. You need to build your customer experience from the ground up on a platform that:

I.   **Engages the digital consumer.** Providing the ability for your customer to engage with your brand over any channel, device, and location—one at a time or all at once, including a phone call. Recognize moments of need or opportunities wherever and whenever they occur.

II. **Engages the digital employee.** Empower your employees to be the CEO of your customers' journeys by using an <u>omnichannel desktop tool</u> to manage all customer interaction types; manage their presence; and drive employee performance, training, and collaboration across the entire enterprise.

III. **Optimizes your digital business.** Use all-channel and device analytics for <u>digital journey optimization</u> and <u>workload management</u> to run your business as a smart business.

<u>https://www.genesys.com/blog/post/growing-problem-of-digital-proliferation-in-the-digital-age</u>

The Power and Perils of Organizational Culture

This reality will extend into the post-pandemic era, where remote working has scattered employees across various locations. Executives need to rethink and leverage cultures.

that will maximize business returns by strengthening their workforce and enhancing the bottom line.

A results-driven culture prioritizes an internal communications strategy and tools that drive engagement and increase retention. Companies with a participative culture see a return on investment that averages twice as high as those with a less participative approach.

In the absolute power scenario, great talent moves first.

This group of people has options, they can find new jobs, work remotely, start their own businesses, or simply leave. In such a culture, there is also the problem of individuals being divided into factions, each led by certain "chiefs." Being labelled as part of a particular faction can mean that, during leadership changes, you might find yourself without a place in the organization. This form of leadership is detrimental; it deprives organizations of valuable talent and skills, and ultimately undermines the bottom line.

How can you dedicate yourself to education and hard work, only to become a 'henchman' in the workplace? This situation is inherently flawed. Remarkably, those in such dictatorial leadership positions often believe they are acting in the organization's best interests. They tend to focus on recounting past victories, believing this will somehow ensure the future sustainability of the business they currently lead. At its core, the absolute power paradigm is rooted in the belief that "I know what's best," and that those I lead would be "lost without my guidance." This mindset fosters the notion of being irreplaceable. The irony, however, is that graveyards are full of people who were once considered "irreplaceable."

Traits of a bad organizational culture include:

I.   Absence of core shared values

II. Lots of gossip in the office

III. Unhealthy employee competition

IV. Absenteeism and tardiness

V.   No time for lunch for the employees and going home late daily.

Leading With Empathy

A strong organizational culture is vital for your company's longevity and success. To build a vibrant culture that attracts job seekers and retains employees, you must be deliberate about the type of organizational culture you want to create. As job seekers gain more leverage in the future, a solid organizational culture will be essential for attracting top talent. To retain these candidates, the key will be employee engagement, which consistently leads to higher productivity.

Organizational culture in the digital age will differ significantly from what it is today, particularly with the post-pandemic shift toward remote and rotational work. In such environments, where employees do not consistently interact with the same people, maintaining a cohesive and engaging culture will be even more challenging.

The Power and Perils of Organizational Culture

To maintain a coherent organizational culture, leadership must commit to ongoing discussions about the organization's purpose, the pivotal role of employees, and the future direction of the company. Leaders need to understand the value of agility and invest in it.

Organizational culture can either be your greatest strength or your most detrimental weakness. The key is to remain vigilant against harmful company culture and work proactively to address and change it. If the organizational culture is unacceptable, employee turnover will likely be high. Employees are often willing to accept a lower salary in a healthier, less toxic environment rather than stay for higher pay in a toxic culture.

The questions to ask yourself are:

Leading With Empathy

I. How prepared was your organization culturally to deal with the crisis?

II. Will the ongoing situation bring your employees together or drive them apart?

III. Will they see the organization differently when this is over?

Your answers will inform what you can achieve in the post-pandemic reality.

7

Being an Effective Boss will Require an Identity Shift

From Novice to Virtuoso: A Guide for First-Time Managers, with an Emphasis on Empathetic Leadership.

We need to guide first-time managers by sharing key insights into what to expect as they embark on their management journey. This role is not just about managing the organization but, more importantly, about leading people. It represents the

Leading With Empathy

first transition from relying solely on IQ and technical capabilities to embracing EQ and integrating individual strengths into a cohesive team. Stepping into a leadership role for the first time is more than a change in tasks; it is a fundamental shift in identity.

Managers must move from doing the work themselves to ensuring that the work is done effectively by others. This transition requires a new level of self-awareness, a broader range of skills, and a fresh perspective on what defines success. Success is now defined by the achievements of your team members, rather than your own individual performance.

I. How can the team achieve the goals of the department or organization?

II. How effective they are as individuals within a team?

Being an Effective Boss will Require an Identity Shift

III. How do they collaborate with colleagues to achieve and complete tasks?

IV. How engaged are the teams on what is expected of them as a collective?

V. How committed is the team to the service for the customer?

VI. Are they motivated and connected?

VII. What culture has been inculcated in the team and the role of the leader?

VIII. What value system is adopted by the team and does the team buy-into it?

The attributes that will make you less effective as a leader are those that focus on self like:

I. My skills

II. My talents

III. My technical know-how

Leading With Empathy

You need to develop a new set of skills in key areas to enable you to lead your team, and the following becomes your new reality:

I.   Mindset shift – Your individual contribution is no longer important.

II.   Relationship building – From peer to boss.

III.   Attitude – Doing all the work by yourself is no longer the goal.

IV.   Perspective – Be politically savvy.

V.   Focus – Realize the importance of integrity and character.

VI.   Skillset – Shift your skillset from technical to influence and team building.

There is no perfect leader, like most skills, the ability to lead must be developed. As a new leader, even with experience, you must gather the resources to learn how to become an effective leader. You must

Being an Effective Boss will Require an Identity Shift

flip from being a great individual contributor to motivating others for success. Communicate with the others, the same way you would want others to communicate with you. Learning to delegate tasks, setting clear goals for everyone is the new name of the game. If you do not delegate, and you do everything by yourself you are sending a message that you do not trust your teams to do a good job, which leads to stagnation and low productivity. This is usually a prescription for disaster.

Navigating Corporate Politics

Every organization has its own unique political landscape, and it is important for new managers to understand the unwritten rules and power dynamics at play. This doesn't mean engaging in unethical or manipulative behavior, but rather being aware of the different stakeholders and their interests, building alliances with key individuals, and learning how to navigate potential conflicts.

As a new leader, you face a significant change in perspective, transitioning from an outsider to an insider and developing an understanding of corporate politics. To be effective, you need to acknowledge that politics are a necessary part of leadership. This involves stepping out of your comfort zone and reaching beyond your current circles to gain diverse insights from people within and outside the organization. This broader perspective helps you navigate and scan the environment effectively. You now face an abrupt change of perspective from being an outsider to being an insider and developing a new sense of understanding of corporate politics. To be an effective leader, it is important to recognize that or-

Being an Effective Boss will Require an Identity Shift

ganizational politics are an inherent aspect of leadership. This is called getting out of your comfort zone and reaching out beyond your current circles, to gain new information from a diverse group of people within and outside of the organization. This gives you a broad perspective to navigate and scan the environment in which you are operating.

Essential to this, is to develop trust and exude integrity, and this comes with time and practice. You need to establish a strong moral code and hold everyone accountable to it. This will help you especially during difficult times. You can achieve this through building trusting relationships with the teams. If you say what you mean and do what you say, you are likely to succeed in your new role and in your career in general.

Leading With Empathy

No one is born a perfect leader; like most skills, leadership must be developed. It is crucial to gather resources to learn how to become effective. Communicate with others the way you would like to be communicated with. Learning to delegate tasks and set clear goals for everyone is key. If you don't delegate and handle everything yourself, you send a message that you don't trust your team, which leads to stagnation and low productivity—often a recipe for disaster.

Building Relationships and Trust through Empathy

Building strong relationships with your team members is essential for effective leadership. Get to know each person as an individual, understand their strengths and weaknesses, and tailor your communication style to their needs. In my mentorship en-

Being an Effective Boss will Require an Identity Shift

deavors, I once mentored one of my first-time managers, she was great at what she did as an individual, so I was helping her navigate the transition. When I asked her if she knows her employees' spouses and children or not, at least their existence, which can assist her to ask about their well-being, she responded that she does not want to pry, so she prefers not to get there. I explained to her the importance of this, as it makes her direct reports feel seen and cared for, she was surprised but in follow up meetings she highlighted how this has impacted her interaction with the team from a productivity perspective. Showing genuine interest in your teams' personal and professional development, creates a safe space where they feel comfortable sharing their ideas and concerns. Trust is the foundation of any successful team. As a new manager, it is important to build transparency and establish trust early on by being reliable, and consistent in your actions. Follow through on your commitments, give credit where it's due, and take responsibility for your mistakes.

Empathy is a critical component of building these strong relationships, understanding your team members' feelings, perspectives, and challenges, creates a more supportive and collaborative environment. This leads to increase motivation, engagement, and productivity. Some specific ways that new managers can demonstrate empathy:

I. **Active listening:** Pay attention to what your team members are saying, both verbally and nonverbally. Ask clarifying questions and reflect what you hear to ensure understanding.

Being an Effective Boss will Require an Identity Shift

II. **Emotional validation:** Acknowledge and validate your team members' feelings, even if you don't necessarily agree with them. Let them know that their emotions are valid and that you care about their well-being.

III. **Perspective-taking:** Try to see things from your team members' point of view. This can help you understand their motivations, concerns, and challenges.

IV. **Offering support:** Provide support and guidance when needed, but also empower your team members to find their own solutions.

V. **Celebrating successes:** Recognize and celebrate the achievements of your team members, both big and small. This can help to boost morale and create a sense of shared accomplishment.

Leading With Empathy

Establish a strong moral code and hold everyone accountable to it. Building trusting relationships with your team is crucial. If you consistently say what you mean and do what you say, you are likely to succeed in your new role and in your career overall.

Humility and self-awareness form part of the critical success factors as a leader. The better you understand yourself and recognize your strengths and weaknesses, the more effective you can be as a leader. These attributes build a reputation that everyone values and desires.

8

The Future of Leadership: Agility and Adaptability

The markets of today and tomorrow will reward agility. Agility in the physical sense is the ability to pivot from one direction to another without losing balance. For an organization, it can be described as the ability for the organization to shape-shift which is driven by willingness of teams to adapt. Establishing a culture that encourages creativity and rapid innovation is the key to success for these young

The Future of Leadership: Agility and Adaptability

teams. Agile leaders will propel their organizations to succeed in the VUCA (Volatile, Uncertain,

Complex, and Ambiguous) world. This requires a shift from the traditional leadership mindset to agile transformational leadership approaches.

In my first leadership role as the East London Port Manager, I quickly realized that the solutions for the challenges I was faced with lie squarely on engagement. To tackle the situation, the focused was on several key strategies:

I. **Market Research and Engagement:** We conducted extensive research to understand the current market demands and identify potential opportunities for the organization. Engaging with local businesses and stakeholders provided valuable insights into what could be done to rejuvenate the business.

II. **Innovation and Adaptation:** Recognizing the need for adaptability, we quickly introduced innovative approaches to diversify our services. This involved exploring new business lines and optimizing existing operations to better meet market needs.

III. **Building Partnerships:** Forming strategic partnerships with key players in the industry helped create synergies that could drive growth. By collaborating with other organizations and stakeholders, we were able to leverage additional resources and expertise.

IV. **Operational Efficiency:** Improving operational processes was crucial. We focused on streamlining operations to reduce costs and enhance efficiency, making the business more competitive.

V. **Communication and Advocacy:** Communicating the value of the business to both internal and external stakeholders was essential. We worked on building a strong case to demonstrate the strategic importance of the turnaround strategy and why they were critical in implementation.

Through these efforts, we were able to stabilize the business operations and set a foundation for future growth. The experience taught me valuable lessons in leadership, adaptability, and strategic thinking, which I've carried forward in my subsequent roles.

Inclusivity as a way of life

The more we used the words "us" and "our" rather than the word "me" the more we gained traction on the way forward. What you would term collective decision-making was at play here. There was a great sense of ownership from all the stakeholders, that came out of this approach. Everyone felt that they were contributing meaningfully to the turnaround strategy, the messages were the same. We also adopted a project management approach in this process, and the success of delivery lay right there. We tackled the Achilles Heels of strategy implementation in our context, head on. We had a series of engagements and conversations sharing and debating ideas on what would be the priority projects, who does what and how does it come together and what would be the key performance areas, so that we could measure our output and impact on customers. This was monitored collectively through a 360degree approach, where there was no scope for anyone to feel better than the rest. We allowed for people to make mistakes in their creativity, and we incentivized great ideas. We were high on engagement on issues and therefore there was a greater level of transparency that built trust.

People play a critical role.

I learnt as I was going along and as the roles were getting tougher, that people are the cornerstone for any business to succeed in a sustainable manner. I must confess that during those early stages of my leadership journey, there were no millennial challenges. I met millennials later in my career, and I was wise enough to read up on them and understand their needs. What I completely mastered at that stage was the importance of employee engagement, that is what we got right. Everyone knew where we were going, everyone knew how we were going to get there, and importantly everyone knew what they were responsible and accountable for to take us there. Leadership was that simple, shared goals and a shared vision, and a set of values and a culture that bind us together. As I progressed in my leadership journey and faced increasingly challenging roles, I learned that people are the cornerstone of any business's sustainable success.

The mindset of future leaders

Soon, the world will be a complex and volatile space to navigate. The geopolitical landscape remains contentious, and on the environmental front, there is a strong push towards green economies and the acceleration of the just energy transition from fossil fuels to green energy. The implementation of technologies like digitization, robotics, AI, IoT, and automation is transforming the workplace, raising concerns about job displacement and the need for upskilling. This disruption brings pressure caused

The Future of Leadership: Agility and Adaptability

by anxiety of job losses from labour unions, on employers, who are seized with the responsibility to develop policies that can manage the labour market and the pressure from society to reduce unemployment.

In this volatile global climate, the future of leadership is rooted in empathy. Future leaders must understand the character, personality, competencies, and conduct of the people they lead. A leader's role is to enable individuals, teams, and organizations to respond quickly and effectively today and to anticipate the challenges of tomorrow, much like a conductor harmonizing an orchestra. Leadership is becoming the best predictor of organizational viability and lasting success. BE READY!

The type of leaders required for the future:

**The Explorer** – Bringing employees and organizations to the unchartered future.

I.   Curious, open to new ideas, agile enough to change direction when hitting a roadblock.

II. Instilling a learning culture in their organizations to adapt otherwise they will lose the competitive edge and will not survive and having a growth mindset.

**The Chef** – balance business, humanity, and technology

I.   People – employee experience, relationships, loyal customers, and social impact

II. Technology – all aspects of how the work gets done, including software devices, and

The Future of Leadership: Agility and Adaptability

automation to bring efficiency, productivity, speed, and decision making.

The Servant – on the ground working with employees in the trenches and lifting people up.

I. Building strong relationships with people above you, building partnerships, and making other people's lives easier

II. Making the employees feel valued and engaged, building strong customer experience, and putting the customers at the center of every decision and most importantly self-care.

The Global Citizen – the world is more connected, every company is global, with customers and employees globally.

I.   You must adopt the mindset of a global citizen taking culture into account and be ready to move – flexibility.

II.   Its more about having a global mindset, respecting diversity of cultures, being open to other people's mindsets, ideas, religions, ethnicities, races, thoughts, and orientations.

Skills required from the leaders of the future.

The Futurist - Look at various possibilities to prepare themselves for what's coming.

Proactively shape the future rather than merely reacting to trends. Look through the cone of possibilities and run through scenarios to envision potential outcomes. Keep an eye on trends and recognize the signs of things to come. It's about exploring multiple paths simultaneously, seeing around many corners to understand what's coming, and choosing the best way forward.

__The Translator__ – ability to communicate and build bridges between people, communicating well into the future, with a clear and concise messaging, using the right channels. Know how to cut through the noise to get people's attention and move them to action. The other side is.

listening deliberately, which is more than hearing, meaning you pay attention to what is being said.

__The Coach__ – you need to be a great coach, and know how to motivate, engage, and inspire people. Be willing to create other leaders, to work across generations and cultures and know how to put together effective teams. Develop employees to be stronger leaders than you. The biggest challenge for future leaders is leading multi-generational work-forces and to understand each group and respect each unique group.

<u>The Technology Teenager</u> – you must be like a teenager, they don't typically read instructions, they don't have to be programmers, they just dive in and try new things. You just need technology fluency and to embrace transformation.

9

Bullying and Toxicity in the Workplace

Always remember that leadership is a privilege. When you are in a leadership role, your influence can significantly impact the trajectories of people's entire careers and often their lives. It is crucial for leaders to understand from the outset that being given the responsibility to lead is not a license to break anyone's spirit. The tendency for some leaders is to assume that being in charge grants them absolute power. This mindset can ruin employee morale and, in turn, damage the organization's prospects for sustainability and profitability. Such a leadership style often results in high employee turnover and a deeply demoralized workforce.

Leaders who bully often do so for two main reasons. First, they feel a need to be seen as competent, which explains the abrasive nature of their leadership. Second, they lack emotional and social intelligence (EQ). Anyone they perceive as a threat to their competence causes them anxiety, which manifests as bullying. They fail to understand the damage their behavior inflicts on others.

Bullies are not psychopaths, and most of them can change with the right tools. They need assistance to understand the negative impact of their behavior on both the individuals they lead and the organizations they manage. Investigating bullying is challenging because it is often intangible. Leaders must recognize the importance of perception and see the need to conduct Employee Health surveys to assess the workplace climate and effect change. Often, accusations of bullying are met with denial or justification. Simply put, bullying is an abuse of power.

There is a stark difference between a tough leader and one who abuses employees. While there is no concrete profile of a bully, all bullies share a need to control and dominate others. It is highly likely that they themselves grew up in environments where vulnerability led to abuse. Their behavior might be a form of self-preservation or a desire for attention, but it manifests in the wrong place and at the expense of others.

Leading With Empathy

Workplace bullying is the repeated mistreatment of employees, often perpetrated by someone in a leadership position. It is a systematic abuse of authority that undermines the working relationship between the bully and their subordinates, ultimately destroying trust within the organization. Bullying causes employees to feel anxious, and depressed, which creates self-doubt, fear, and anger.

Bullies can be either male or female, but both are more likely to target women at work. When bullying is allowed to persist without consequences, by the time it is detected, the company would have already lost significant value through the departure of good employees and the erosion of skills.

Bullying and Toxicity in the Workplace

"A bad leader can kill a good process" Rixio Madina.

Bullying can be embedded in every area of a business, from the C-Suite to the front lines. Employees are often afraid to report bullying by their bosses because of the risk of losing their jobs, damaging their careers and reputations, and compromising their financial security. As a result, many choose to endure it. Bullying is the kryptonite of success and innovation; it hurts people and, most importantly, it hurts the organization's bottom line. It leads to absenteeism, high staff turnover, and lost productivity. Additionally, it incurs monetary losses through legal cases and erodes employee trust and loyalty.

Bullying creates a toxic working environment with reduced levels of trust, making it difficult to attract new talent as the organization's reputation suffers. Poor team dynamics caused by a lack of trust result in low productivity and morale, leading to exceptionally low-quality customer service. Statistics show that 46% of people believe bullying adversely impacts their work performance and negatively affects their mental health. Moreover, 28% of employees take time off work due to bullying. Bullying leads to minimal performance, with employees doing just enough to get by.

10

A Personal Reflection on Bullying

After holding several incredible leadership positions, I felt an ardent desire to make a difference at the Passenger Rail Agency of South Africa (PRASA). PRASA faced monumental challenges, including vandalized infrastructure and non-operational trains, which starkly contrasted with the state-of-the-art infrastructure and rolling stock of the Gautrain.

A Personal Reflection on Bullying

When I received the call inviting me to consider the position of rail CEO at PRASA, my initial reaction was to quell my silent desire to take on the challenge. However, it's important for me to articulate what ultimately encouraged me to take this brave step, despite the voices of the naysayers.

At the time, PRASA was under administration, led by Bongisizwe Mpondo, whom I did not know well at the time. Nevertheless, his public presentations on the rail recovery plan inspired my confidence. It was clear to me that he was a man with a well-defined strategy to turn around the passenger railways. I realized that joining such a leader to operationalize this strategy and provide the much-needed rail transport for commuters would be a significant contribution. Mpondo was consistently on national television and in parliament, clearly articulating his turnaround strategy for PRASA. There was no ambiguity about his vision; he communicated it very well.

In my mind, here was a leader who had thoroughly analyzed the needs and resources required to move the business forward. I felt he needed effective implementers to execute the strategy. This approach, coupled with my desire to test the practical solutions I had learned while running the Gautrain and the simplified global best practices I had observed whilst working in the Paris railway system, motivated me. Additionally, the context for me was that passenger rail is the single most affordable mode of transport for daily commuters.

With these considerations, I decided to take on the challenge at PRASA, driven by the belief that we

A Personal Reflection on Bullying

could make a substantial difference in providing reliable rail transport.

So, I joined PRASA in the middle of the pandemic. As I already indicated, there had been no trains running for more than a year, and this situation predated the pandemic. On June 17th, 2020, during the lockdown, I decided to take on the challenge. When I got there, I was briefed that the first corridor must be operational by the 30 June 2020, in a railway system that did not have any overhead lines, security, stations were vandalised, and the copper was stolen in every corridor, making it impossible to run electric trains. We started working on a diesel train solution to meet the target dates, and we de-electrified the first corridor. The first thing you do as a leader in an environment like this is to build strong teams and set a clear vision and mission with well-defined objectives. So, we began with the process.

The teams were motivated, and we encouraged a collaborative environment where hierarchy was minimised. We met the deadline of June 30, 2024, to launch the first corridor, and our political leaders rode the train in disbelief. We then rolled out our train corridor plan across the country, and in exactly eight months, we had launched 11 Metrorail corridors in total across all four regions. We also launched the 7 long-distance Shosholoza Mail trains nationwide, parallel to this process. In total we had launched 18 corridors in that short space of time.

We were delivering an excellent service under very challenging circumstances, but the focus and coordination of our cross-functional teams—from the executives responsible for security, engineering,

A Personal Reflection on Bullying

train stations, the buses, which served as our backup plan for long-distance trains— we worked like a well-rehearsed orchestra. In Mpondo, we had an amazing leader who allowed us the freedom to do what we needed and provided the support required to achieve PRASA's key objectives. Although we didn't have abundant operational budgets, we had our teams to make things happen.

At this point, the Administrator was released for reasons beyond our control, which I won't dwell on here as it's not the focus of this book. Perhaps one day, Mpondo will write about the subject and the behind-the-scenes details.

At the end of September, an interim Accounting Officer was appointed. The new Accounting Officer listened to presentations from the executives and was convinced our plans were solid. He gave us the

Leading With Empathy

space and support to carry on with the implementation plan. Unfortunately, he only stayed for one month, another complicated process. No one could have imagined what was yet to come after his departure.

A month later, a permanent new Board was appointed and subsequently an interim Group CEO was put in place. With any change in leadership, there is always an expectation that things will change, and it is wise to anticipate this. No one would have imagined what that meant. Indeed, things changed drastically. All hell broke loose!!

This period was marked by abuse and bullying from the very beginning. We were relentlessly browbeaten for reasons that remain unclear, especially by someone who had been part of the turnaround from

A Personal Reflection on Bullying

day one. We expected that our plan would be understood and properly communicated to the new Board. We also hoped to be given the opportunity to explain to the Board where we had started and just how dire the situation had been when we took over.

However, the Board had no time to listen to the executive team, and many wrong assumptions were made about the state of affairs. It felt as though we were considered enemies of the state without any real reason. Sadly, we may never understand why this was happening. We are left with more questions than answers.

The level of abuse and toxicity in the environment reached such a height that we were shouted at daily. We were not allowed to make suggestions, as this was seen as competing with our principal for the position. Time was wasted on issues unrelated to delivery, focusing instead on managing boardroom politics. We were asked questions by some of the new members that left us gobsmacked, things like why we don't advertise the trains like Nando's does adverts, to why the trains are not moving by-directional at the same time when we had a single line, I was not sure whether the return trains were expected to fly.

This unbearable period lasted only four months, but it felt like four years. It was characterized by favouritism and pure hatred. The amount of fear instilled in the system was overwhelming. If I were to recount some of the stories, you might think I was exaggerating.

Then the plotting began, we were subjected to what seemed like a performance management process for

A Personal Reflection on Bullying

the second quarter since our arrival. Remember, the first performance management was linked to our initial performance and supposedly probation period. This was conducted by the same leader in Human Resources at the time and was now evaluating us as our principal. During the three-month probation period, our performance scores were excellent. We had performed well, although this wasn't formally linked to probation.

In the second round of so-called performance management, however, we were suddenly deemed the worst performers. This evaluation was based on arbitrary criteria, such as why we had interviews with the Sunday Times to why we were on the radio discussing rail performance. To clarify, it is standard protocol for CEOs of divisions to respond to these questions through the Communications department.

Leading With Empathy

This happens all the time and is part of the job. But here it was a trigger of sorts, it touched some nerves. There was a particular Sunday Times coverage that was organised by Makhosini Mgitywa our Communications executive with the Sunday Times. It was an excellent coverage of what we are doing to bring rail back, a very positive article. I still think this article was viewed as "you want my job" kind of article. It never left the performance discussions.

We had established a routine of visiting stations and riding the trains in the mornings to ensure that service was being properly executed and that our passengers were receiving good service. February 18, 2021, was no different. We were visiting Pretoria station after getting off a train. We had breakfast with Board members who were on a site visit, and

A Personal Reflection on Bullying

we were preparing to join them to update them on our progress.

Suddenly, we were informed that the Acting Group CEO wanted to see us in one of the offices of the bus CEO, which is located at Pretoria station. We went there, thinking we would discuss our approach with the Board in preparation for the site visit. When we arrived, we were told to come in one at a time. It was myself and my colleague from the technical division.

To my shock, a brown A4-sized envelope was placed in front of me, and I was told, "Sorry, Ms. Damasane, you have not made it, so this is the end of the road." Confused, I asked, "I have not made it for what?" The response was, "Probation!" Still bewildered by what this meant, I was then asked to leave immediately. This situation was supposed to

be painful—being fired and for not making probation – effectively so-called non-performance—but
instead, I felt a huge sense of relief. There is no
measure of what abuse does to the mental health of
a human being, not even a good paycheque.

We left the station and PRASA, and the rest is history. We fought the case in court and won, as we
should have. My intentions were more about clear-
ing my name than returning to the company. Once I
achieved that, I moved on with my life. It was en-
couraging, albeit after the effect for some board
members to apologise for being complicit in such a
decision, at the time, claiming they were new and
believed what they were told.

11

Strategies for Building a Bully-Free Workplace

Reputation is closely tied to culture. Some organizations establish a compact with their employees based on a set of agreed-upon values that govern how things are done, which constitutes their organizational culture. The organizations that successfully attract and retain great talent are those that "walk the talk" regarding their culture. Employees in these organizations feel positive about their work and are often fully aligned with the values espoused.

The beliefs and values that guide behavior in an organization might seem intangible, but culture is inextricably linked to the organization's bottom line. At the heart of a high-performance culture is a communication strategy that centres on the workplace. Great leaders view culture as a strategic priority rather than allowing it to evolve passively. They understand that culture is a defining element of the workplace experience. The key is to ensure that every employee feels important and included.

My own experience with bullying at PRASA was a stark reminder of the devastating impact that toxic leadership can have on individuals and organizations. Despite the initial success of our efforts, the subsequent change in leadership and the ensuing

Strategies for Building a Bully-Free Workplace

culture of bullying and intimidation derailed our progress and created a hostile work environment.

This experience taught me the importance of not only advocating for an empathetic leadership culture and actively working to prevent and address bullying in the workplace. It reinforced my belief that a positive and supportive workplace culture is essential for both employee well-being and organizational success.

By sharing my story, I hope to raise awareness of the issue of workplace bullying and encourage others to speak out against it. It is time for leaders to take a stand against this harmful behavior and create workplaces where everyone feels safe, valued, and empowered to reach their full potential.

It is becoming evident that more leaders are bullies and misinterpret the appointment as a passport to rule people's lives as they please, and tend to think the organization is their home, so they do what they like, the way they like it.

The features of the bullying tactics that led to the firing resembled the following:

I.   **Intimidation**: Creating a fearful work environment through threats and aggressive behavior.

II. **Verbal Attacks/Shouting**: Using loud and aggressive communication to dominate and belittle employees.

III. **False Accusations**: Making baseless claims to discredit and undermine employees.

IV. **Overruling Decisions**: Disregarding and overturning employees' decisions and contributions without justification.

Creating a bully-free environment

Creating a bully-free workplace requires a multifaceted approach and the commitment of everyone in the organization. Organizations can take proactive steps to address and prevent bullying in the workplace.

Some strategies that can be implemented.

I. **Taking Feedback Seriously**: Actively listening to employees' concerns and taking appropriate action.

II. **Establishing Policies that Promote a Positive Company Culture**: Developing clear guidelines that define acceptable behavior and consequences for violations.

III. **Having a Corrective Action Policy**: Implementing procedures to address and rectify instances of bullying.

IV. **Engaging Experts in Training and Coaching**: Utilizing professional resources to educate and support employees and leaders.

V. **Leadership Accountability**: Leaders must be held accountable for their behavior and create a culture of respect and inclusivity. This involves modelling positive behavior, addressing any instances of bullying promptly and effectively, and creating a safe space for employees to report concerns without fear of retaliation.

VI. **Engaging Experts in Training and Coaching**: Provide training for leaders and employees on how to identify and address bullying behavior. This can include workshops, seminars, and online resources that educate employees about the different forms of bullying, the impact it can have on individuals and the organization, and how to respond to it effectively.

VII. **Support for Victims**: Offer counselling and support services to employees who have been bullied. This can help them cope with the emotional and psychological impact of bullying and provide them with the resources they need to heal and move forward.

VIII. **Zero Tolerance**: Enforce a zero-tolerance policy for bullying, with clear consequences for perpetrators. This sends a strong message that bullying will not be tolerated and creates a culture of accountability.

IX. **Open Communication**: Encourage open and honest communication about workplace bullying. Create a safe space where employees feel comfortable sharing their experiences and concerns without fear of retaliation. Providing training to improve interpersonal communication skills.

X. **Promote a Positive Workplace Culture**: Foster a positive workplace culture that values respect, collaboration, and inclusivity. This can be achieved through team-building activities, recognition programs, and initiatives that promote employee well-being.

Creating a bully-free workplace requires a multi-faceted approach and the commitment of everyone in the organization. Implementing these strategies, can assist organizations to create a workplace where everyone feels safe, valued, and respected. This not

Strategies for Building a Bully-Free Workplace

only benefits employees but also contributes to a more productive, innovative, and successful organization.

12

Sharing Leadership Experiences

I have felt a deep sense of obligation to write about leaders who do not understand the consequences of their leadership styles on people's lives, livelihoods, and families. I hope that some readers will learn from this book and strive to do better, avoiding certain pitfalls as they grow into their own leadership roles. This book is meant for future leaders to learn the dos and don'ts of effective leadership.

Leading With Empathy

With over 25 years of experience in leadership roles, I have often been accused of collective decision-making, over-consulting, involving everyone too much, and being too inclusive. I have even been labelled a "people pleaser." However, in the post-pandemic world, the collective management approach is something we will all need to adopt. Let's assume these labels fit my description—what is wrong with that concept? I would rather live with this label than that of a toxic leader. Funny enough earlier we spoke about being a tough leader does not imply an abuser. Working through and with people will always be a winner as they are keen to work 24/7 for your organisation. This leadership style builds a sense of ownership.

I find comfort in embracing the people I lead; it gets things done and makes people feel seen and heard. Not once have I felt that this approach diminishes my ability to make tough decisions when necessary. Someone once asked me, "So, I hear that your strength is people management?" as if this was a weakness in terms of content knowledge, as if I knew nothing else. My response was, "Yes, I work extremely well with people. I feel that leadership is about that, and it is a great bonus that you have the expertise and experience to do the technical work. As discussed earlier, being a firm leader does not equate to being abusive.

To get things done, you need people. People need to feel like they know you and that they can trust you. You need to give yourself authentically; there is no other way. Their voices are as critical as yours; it's not a highway from top to bottom, NO. Inclusive leadership, respect, communication, and teamwork improve at all levels of employment. This inspires people to develop the most needed skills in the workplace: adaptability, agility, learning, partnering, authenticity, and, most importantly, a growth mindset.

I believe communication is the biggest value that can be attributed to the success of an entity. For strategy execution to succeed, a leader needs "all on board." This gives everyone better accountability and ownership. When teams have candid conversations about their strengths and weaknesses, they can identify how best to bridge their gaps and achieve their goals. That openness only happens when managers take the time to build an environment of safety and trust.

Another important aspect is talent optimization, which is the art of championing self-awareness, empowering people to bring their best selves to work.

Sharing Leadership Experiences

Turnover won't slow overnight, but by demonstrating your commitment to your people each day, you'll surely see the momentum shift.

In conclusion, organizational culture is the backbone of any successful enterprise, defining its character and shaping the behavior and attitudes of its members. By fostering an environment of trust, care, and transparency, leaders can inspire their employees to achieve their best and align with the organization's vision.

The post-pandemic world has underscored the importance of empathetic leadership, where collective decision-making, inclusivity, and genuine engagement are not just preferable but essential. Leaders who adapt to these principles will find themselves better equipped to navigate the complexities of

Leading With Empathy

modern business and foster a thriving, motivated workforce.

Talent retention is a critical outcome of a strong organizational culture. When employees feel valued, respected, and part of a cohesive team, they are more likely to remain committed to the organization. This sense of belonging and purpose not only reduces turnover but also enhances overall productivity and morale. Investing in people and creating a supportive environment, will ensure that organizations attract and retain top talent, driving long-term success and innovation.

By sharing my experiences and the lessons I've learned, I hope to inspire future leaders to embrace these values and avoid the pitfalls of toxic leadership. Remember, effective leadership is not about exerting power but about empowering others. As we

Sharing Leadership Experiences

move forward, let us commit to building cultures
where everyone feels valued, heard, and motivated
to contribute to shared success.

THANK YOU!

I am always grateful to my parents, when writing gets tough, I am reminded of my late dad, smoking his cigarette while working on his books. That memory gives me the energy to continue: my late mom's tenacity, strong will, and soft touch.

Nomava and Ayabulela, my creative children, thank you for always trusting my decisions as I steer our lives. It is a great honour to be your mother. Without Jesus as our Lord and Savior, our lives would have turned out very differently. Thank you for the time dedicated to my writing and your creativity Nomava.

I would also like to convey my appreciation to my extended family, particularly Mrs. Nambitha Stofile, for co-mothering with me where I am lacking. S'Nambi, the mother of my housemate Sive Stofile, who has been like a third daughter to me, has shown immense love and support during the difficult periods of my life. Your presence has been a great comfort, especially during my PRASA days when you all endured the worst with me.

Sandra Burmeister and Nerine Kahn for the amazing legal, emotional and all the support and guidance they gave during this difficult period.

Lastly, thank you to Sihlangule Siwisa for the final read and for smoothing out some of the thorny parts of this book.

With gratitude